Letters at Christmas

Inspiration from Paul and Cicero

Gerald O'Collins, SJ, AC

Published by Connor Court Publishing, 2024.

CONNOR COURT PUBLISHING PTY LTD
PO Box 7257
Redland Bay QLD 4165
sales@connorcourt.com

www.connorcourtpublishing.com.au

Cover design: Maria Giordano

ISBN: 9781923224315

Printed in Australia

This book is dedicated to the Jesuit Faber Community (Parkville, Australia) with whom I have been privileged to spend my final years.

Contents

Preface

Do Christmas letters and cards read the divine presence in the year that is closing down and express gratitude for being set on paths of peace and happiness? Does such mail imply that our faith in the Lord allows us to sort out, cope with, and even rejoice in what has happened to us and our dear ones?

Jesus is not merely the right answer. He is the living answer who invests everything with meaning. We don't have to depend on ourselves anymore. With him we can work through everything.

The end of some years can leave us flooded with love and joy. Such Christmas good news filled out the letter to me from one cousin. Far from continuing to struggle with health issues and the loss of loved ones, she wrote of weddings and christenings—of aunties and grandmothers "fighting for cuddles when Leah was born."

We know also how deep undercurrents of unresolved problems and failures to forgive can leave families torn apart. Christmas may see us as perplexed and even shocked as ever by the destructive forces that invade our closest relationships and the wider scene.

One life-long, Italian friend has spent decades working for the European Union and other such institutions, and finds that they have "failed dramatically to enhance peace efforts." She even felt that they "are just supporting war, more war, more war, and more war and war preparation." A 2023 Christmas letter summed up her feelings:

> I often wondered what my later years on earth would be like, and never thought of such a scenario—witnessing genocide here and there, with very few reactions. I hear Pope Francis saying wise things, but deaf ears fail to receive his messages. It is very hard to find a reason to survive all this, and impossible, at least now, to enjoy anything, while thinking how much suffering happens all around.

This book presents fifteen Christmas letters that I composed and sent out from 2009 to 2023. Over those years, more than ever I have been gratefully aware of how much I have personally owed to the apostle Paul and drawn from his letters to constantly inspire my life of faith. He belongs to the living sources of what I wrote.

Seven of his letters, written between 50 AD and the early sixties (Romans, 1 Corinthians, 2 Corinthians, Galatians, Philippians, 1 Thessalonians, and Philemon) are widely agreed to go back to Paul and not derive (like the pastoral letters to Timothy and Titus) from disciples of the apostle. Since Jesus died and rose from the dead around 30 AD, those seven certainly authentic letters predate the Gospels (first Mark in the late sixties and then the works of the other three evangelists). Paul emerges as easily the first major witness to faith in Jesus Christ the Son of God, and does so through his letters.

What the apostle Paul wrote has rubbed off on my vision of Catholic Christianity. He always seemed a trustworthy guide, and his letters brought me into direct contact with him and his Jesus-centered message.

This volume recalls some of the major thrusts of the apostle's teaching before moving to fifteen Christmas letters I have composed. Readers can decide for themselves which Pauline themes shine through what I wrote to family and friends at Christmas.

My thanks go out to Connor Court Publishing for permission to reproduce in an epilogue some reflections on writing letters, and to Stephanie MacGillivray (and *The Pastoral Review*) for permission to reprint in an appendix her review of my *Letters to Maev: A Theologian and His Sister* (Brisbane, Australia: Connor Court Publishing, 2023).

To introduce each Christmas letter, I have added a suitable prayer from the 1998 English translation of the sacramentary prepared by the International Commission on English in the Liturgy (ICEL) and rejected by powerful forces at the Vatican. ICEL's superb version was replaced by the oddly Latinized English of the 2010 official translation and imposed on Catholics of the Roman Rite. With John Wilkins, I told the story of this takeover in *Lost in Translation* (Collegeville, MN: Liturgical Press, 2017). The richly nourishing prayers of the 1998 sacramentary show themselves to be such when supplementing the texts of the Christmas letters. It can only be at our serious loss that these prayers remain archived and unused.

Gerald O'Collins, Faber Community, Parkville, Victoria.

10

1

Lasting Influences of Paul's Letters

The life of Christian believers, in its origins and continuance, remains unthinkable without letters. Faith in Jesus has always involved the presence of others. It was never confined to a closed place for "me" and Jesus alone. St Paul assures his readers: "I believed and so I spoke" (2 Cor 4:13); and we might add, "and so I wrote." His correspondence continued to bring about his apostolic presence to others, even while he remained physically absent.

Letters of Paul

After Paul pioneered the writing of letters by Christians, he would be followed by a sparkling cast that included such figures as Ignatius of Antioch (d. 107 AD), Egeria the pilgrim (probably fourth century), Augustine of Hippo (d. 430), Symeon the New Theologian (d. 1022), Ignatius Loyola (d. 1556), John Henry Newman (d. 1890), Dietrich Bonhoeffer (d. 1945), Helmuth James von Moltke (d. 1945), Sister Wendy Beckett (d. 2018), and innumerable others. The apostle's letters had already put on display at least four relevant characteristics.

First, this correspondence calls on its readers to follow Christ who has died by crucifixion, and risen to a new and glorious life: "He was handed over for our sins and rose again for our justification" (Rom 4:25). This centrality of the passion and resurrection (1 Cor 2:2; 15:1–11) in Paul's mindset does not however dislodge the birth of Jesus from its place in the apostle's message. He was born of the Blessed Virgin Mary (Gal 4:4). We know him as the Messiah "descended from David according to the flesh" (Rom 1:3).

The apostle's faith embraces both Bethlehem and Calvary, both the incarnation and the redemption through crucifixion and resurrection. Some artists, like Matthias Grünewald on the Isenheimer altar expressed this "both/and" by the swaddling clothes of the Christ Child. Our Lady holds her Son in the same cloth he will later wear on the cross.

Second, from the earliest examples, heartfelt *thanksgiving* for what life in Christ has already brought characterizes the apostle's letters. He constantly remembers before God the "work of faith and the labor of love and steadfastness of hope" that the Thessalonians have displayed (1 Thes 1:3). In their Christian life, Paul recognizes the abundant presence of the good news which they have embraced (1 Thes 1:2–16) and expresses deep gratitude for what he discerns.

"Christianity," the Australian priest-poet Peter Steele wrote, "is essentially a religion of the local and specific."[1] Time and again, the apostle Paul slows down to express thanks for what he has experienced in and through particular events that have nourished him, like the way

---

[1] P. Steele, *A Local Habitation: Poems and Homilies* (Parkville, Australia: Newman College, 2011), 3.

his collaborator Titus has not only healed relations between the apostle and the Corinthian community but also inspired their generosity in contributing funds to the impoverished Christians of the mother church in Jerusalem.[2]

Third, such gratitude for the past underpins a powerful *hope* for the future. Experiencing in the incarnated and resurrected Son the presence of God to us and for us empowers Paul to work through anything.

Fourth, what we hear of Epaphroditus (Phil 2:25–30; 4:18) illustrates how an unexpected crisis shaped the context of the apostle's letter to the congregation of Philippi. Epaphroditus had risked his life to visit Paul (who was being held in a jail), fell ill, and almost died. What Paul wrote about this close collaborator put on display the *revelatory* nature of such correspondence. It reveals the love that prompts such authors into writing and unveiling the deepest feelings that bind them to those with whom they communicate. They are "friends" to whom they trustingly disclose themselves.

We have listed four characteristics of Paul's correspondence, characteristics that continue to show up in the life of Christian disciples and not least in the letters exchanged when recalling the birth of Jesus in Bethlehem. (1) They presuppose a shared following of the incarnated and resurrected Son of God; (2) deep gratitude makes them letters of thanksgiving; (3) they construct a basis to hope for life here and hereafter; (4) they are nothing less than acts of self-revelation prompted by love.

---

[2]   G. O'Collins, *Facing up to Jesus in the Gospels and Paul* (Brisbane, Australia: Connor Court Publishing. 2023), 133–36.

This list never intends to describe fully the apostle's correspondence, let alone what it might mean that the literary record of the Church's origins begins with his letters. Rather I am simply sketching a case for the apostle Paul being understood as the patron of Christian letters—specifically, those exchanged at the season of Christmas.

Against that background we now present fifteen letters, which witness at Christmas to the blessings of the year and the inspiration they have radiated. Telling that history with gratitude will not make us miraculously immune from challenges, but its outcome could be greater generosity in following the newborn Christ Child.

2

Christmas 2009

"Eternal God, every year you gladden our hearts by renewing our hope of redemption.

Grant that we who accept your only Son as our Redeemer may face him with confidence when he comes as our judge.

He lives and rules with you in the unity of the Holy Spirit, God for ever and ever."

Prayer for the vigil of Christmas.

The BIG event of 2009 was relocating the base of my ministry from Wimbledon to the Jesuit Theological College in the Melbourne suburb of Parkville. The college, which consists of ten terrace houses built in the late nineteenth century, faces Royal Parade, a spacious avenue shaped by lines of elms and heading north towards Sydney. My office, on the first floor, looks through the trees at the traffic and across to the tennis courts of University College. A bedroom at the back (also on the first floor) opens up glimpses of trees and shrubs and the playing fields of Royal Park. Birds galore hang around everywhere: magpies, wattle birds, mud larks, butcher birds, parrots of various persuasions, willy wagtails (fantail flycatchers) and some assorted imports, like blackbirds, Indian mynahs, pigeons, doves, and the occasional sparrow.

In September I left London with a bang—with two weddings and a funeral. The editor of *The Tablet*, Catherine Pepinster, hosted a dinner after my Tablet Lecture was delivered, the reception ended, and the captains, kings, and princesses had departed.

Writing has not stopped. Next March, Oxford University Press will publish *Jesus Our Priest*, an ecumenical study of the priesthood of Christ, co-authored with Revd Michael Jones, a parish priest who lives in Connecticut and near Yale University.

"Pilgrimages" will also continue: the first involves chairing a meeting (of theologians and scientists) for the Templeton Foundation in Oxford (at the Randolph Hotel) 15-17 April, 2010.[3] The theme is "Light from Light," and Eerdmans (Grand Rapids, Michigan) seem interested in publishing the proceedings.

When a Templeton Foundation representative phoned to invite me to chair the proceedings, I explained: "Yes, I will gladly accept, provided Sir John Polkinghorne is coming." "He is coming," I was told, "and he suggested your name."[4]

A very happy and blessed Christmas and New Year to you and all your dear ones.

---

[3]   *Inspector Morse*, a popular TV show (1987–2000), set a detective and his trusted co-worker on the trail of criminal cases in and around Oxford University. The cases took them not only to the colleges but also inside a sumptuous, period hotel, the Randolph.

[4]   A leading theoretical physicist, John Polkinghorne (1930–2021) was ordained an Anglican priest and became a significant writer on issues of science and faith.

3

Christmas 2010

"God of Abraham and Sarah, of David and his descendants, untiring is your love for us and steadfast your covenant.

Wonderful beyond words is your gift of the Savior, born of the Virgin Mary.

Count us among the people in whom you delight, and by this night's marriage of earth and heaven draw all generations into the embrace of your love.

We ask this through Jesus Christ, your Word made flesh, who lives and rules with you in the unity of the Holy Spirit, in the splendor of eternal light, God for ever and ever."

Prayer for the vigil of Christmas

.

As the year moves towards its close, the year sorts itself out and the landmark events of 2010 become clearer. For myself and my family, the death of Jim Peters at the age of 96 marked the year. A very handsome medic, he had served in the siege of Tobruk and at the battle of El Alamein. Military service in North Africa provided him with glimpses of Evelyn Waugh and the eccentric characters who create and confuse Waugh's wartime novels.

Soon after being discharged from the army, Jim married my eldest sister Moira in early 1946. As a teenage boy at the wedding reception, I was given the task of chatting with an elderly lady festooned with pearls and diamonds. Her husband had made a fortune out of gold mines. They had no children, if I remember rightly, and she finished her days being cared for by Carmelite sisters. As a leading surgeon (urologist), the husband of my wonderful sister, and father of eight children, Jim remained a huge presence in the life of the whole family. His passing to God on 28 September seemed like the going forth of a Viking king from his people. We called him "Big Jim" and he deserved that name.

During 2010, I continued to travel: in April to chair a meeting (on science and faith) in Oxford for the Templeton Foundation; mid-July to mid-August (right after the World Cup) to deliver lectures in South Africa (in Johannesburg, Bloemfontein, Cape Town, and Durban); and then back to the USA in early October (to lecture in San Francisco, New York and Newport, Rhode Island). During the year I kept up publishing: with Mike Jones, *Jesus Our Priest* (Oxford University Press), *Philip Pullman's Jesus* (Darton, Longman & Todd/Paulist Press), and (with two friends) Anthony de Mello's lectures on the Spiritual Exercises of St Ignatius Loyola, published by Doubleday as *Seek God Everywhere*. That publication was made more demanding, but ultimately more rewarding, by an exigent New York editor who had found, or rather been found by, Jesus through reading de Mello some years earlier.

I continue to be astonished and deeply grateful for all the kindness experienced on a big scale or a small scale. In mid-September two

English friends conspired to give me my first visit to the Sydney Opera House—to attend a dazzling performance of Verdi's *Rigoletto*. When I entered the USA on 30 September, the official on passport control decided that, since we were both of Irish origin and shared the same name, there was no need to photograph and fingerprint me. He instantly stamped my passport and waved me on. A month later, back in Melbourne, the governor of Victoria asked me to dine with Emperor Hirohito's daughter, now 71 and on a visit with her husband to Melbourne for the BIG race meeting, the Melbourne Cup. She turned out to be very gracious and charming, But she was disappointed, as, unlike two years ago, a Japanese horse failed to win. A French horse, ridden by a French jockey, took the honours.

Every blessing and grace at Christmas and in the New Year.

4

Christmas 2011

"Lord our God, we celebrate with joy the birth of our Redeemer.

Grant that through worthy and holy lives, we may be welcomed into his glorious company for ever."

Prayer for the vigil of Christmas.

This past year took me away from Melbourne on various occasions: once to Lismore in Northern New South Wales (for lectures to fifty people in education) and once to Perth (for lectures at the University of Western Australia). In August, the Templeton Foundation was flew me over to Denmark for a meeting of fourteen theologians and scientists (on the incarnation) held very close to Hamlet's castle in Elsinore. From our hotel, Marienlyst (which was also the first casino to open in Denmark), we watched a thunder storm break over the castle and saw lightning flashing around the battlements. Statues of Hamlet and Vikings dot the landscape in those parts.

A cousin, Naomi Harbison, with her Danish husband and two teenage boys, gave the visit a family glow. They brought me from Marienlyst to their home and spent two days showing me Copenhagen and its environs. I have known Naomi since the days when she was growing up in Black Rock (Dublin) as the fourth child of Jock and Eleanor Harbison. She was always delightful company and has become even more so, year by passing year. Her husband works for the shipping company Maersk.

For better or worse, I continue to publish, with the latest major book being *Rethinking Fundamental Theology* (Oxford University Press). In very early 2012 Paulist Press (Mahwah, NJ) will put out my *Believing in the Resurrection*, probably my last book on the subject. At this stage of life, I am more concerned about the practice of resurrection than its theory.

For their Christmas number, the London *Tablet* seems to have decided on publishing a piece I wrote on Jesus fiction (read Philip Pullman. Since I began contributing to the *Tablet* at Easter 1968, it's about time to stop.

A lasting link with the journal began when Tom Burns, the editor of this weekly wrote to request an article about the resurrection. "Tom," I pleaded, "I'm lying low in my college, and desperately trying to finish writing my doctoral thesis for the Cambridge divinity faculty." He replied by indicating the date when he expected my text.

Every blessing now to you and all your dear ones at Christmas and in the New Year.

5

Christmas 2012

"God our Creator, you made this most holy night radiant with the splendor of the one true light.

Grant in your mercy that, as we celebrate on earth the mystery of that light, we may also rejoice in its fullness in heaven."

Prayer for Midnight Mass at Christmas.

Here in the Southern hemisphere, students and colleagues are departing for summer assignments and holidays. One [Michael Smith, SJ] has headed south to Antarctica and will spend a month as a chaplain on an Australian base. He hopes to include a quick visit to the South Pole.[5] Some like it cold! Celebrating a wedding for two friends on 29 December will close the year out for me.

On 11 October, the feast of Blessed [now Saint] John XXIII, Catholics and others recalled how fifty years ago he opened the Second Vatican Council (1962–65). That anniversary has involved me in speaking at conferences (in Sydney and Melbourne) and in two weeks of lecturing in the UK for the diocese of Portsmouth and also (one lecture) for Heythrop College (London). I have written articles on Vatican II for

---

[5]   In the event, Michael celebrated the Eucharist for a congregation at the south pole.

various journals: *America, The Pastoral Review, The Tablet,* and *Theological Studies.* There is more to come! In March 2013, Oxford University Press will publish my *The Second Vatican Council on Other Religions.*

In July, Connor Court (Victoria) (with Gracewing, Leominster) published volume one of my memoirs, *A Midlife Journey.* The former Archbishop of Canterbury, George Carey, contributed a generous foreword. Volume two, covering 1974-2006 and entitled *On the Left Bank of the Tiber,* will follow soon, also published by Connor Court.

The knights and dames of the Order of Malta keep me busy as a magistral chaplain (celebrating Masses, leading their annual retreat, and providing the anointing of the sick). The Grand Master, Matthew Festing, visited Melbourne briefly and encouraged members of the Order and others (especially young people) to work for those in need.

Some supervision (two long research essays, a master's thesis, and several doctorates) keeps afloat my teaching life. The students are all doing degrees for the MCD University of Divinity.

This year has seen some cherished friends, Cardinal Carlo Maria Martini, Father Peter Steele, and Alec Lynch, go off to God. I wrote obituaries for each of them—in Martini's case, obituaries for three journals. [These obituaries also appeared in my *Portraits*: *Popes, Family, and Friends* (Brisbane, Australia: Connor Court, 2019).]

Every blessing for Christmas and the New Year from the newborn Savior...

6

Christmas 2013

"Good and gracious God, on this holy night you gave us your Son, the Lord of the universe, wrapped in swaddling clothes, the Savior of all, lying in a manger. On this holy night draw us into the mystery of your love.

Join our voices with the heavenly host, that we may sing your glory on high.

Give us a place among the shepherds, that we may find the One for whom we have waited, Jesus Christ, your Word made flesh, who lives and rules with you in the unity of the Holy Spirit, in the splendor of eternal light, God for ever and ever."

Prayer for Midnight Mass.

As usual, the year has been punctuated with trips to give lectures: in northern New South Wales, South Australia, and Western Australia, as well as trips within Victoria (to Bacchus Marsh and Bendigo). Bacchus Marsh gave me a fascinating entrée into country life in that district, as my brief was to speak at a breakfast attended by various Christians on the occasion of Father's Day.

Occupying the Jesuit chair at St Thomas More College in Perth opened up invitations from several departments of the University of Western Australia. The philosophy department did not want to hear of me, but the English departure engaged me to speak on the interpretation of the Holy Trinity in the poetry of John Donne (d. 1631). The fine arts specialty, housed within architecture, wanted me to present an illustrated lecture on episodes in the story of Jesus. For the history department I could develop suggestions for healthy research—a task made easier by my own work in producing a life of my grandfather Patrick McMahon Glynn (Melbourne University Press and Cambridge University Press) and further historical publications. Research in theology must constantly grapple with biblical and Christian history. Constructing a non-historical theology would embody an escape from the truth.

On the local scene here in Melbourne, I continue to celebrate the Eucharist, offer spiritual retreats, and do other things for the Knights and Dames of Malta. One of them, Richard Divall, the only fully professed Knight of Malta in Australia, has just submitted a doctoral dissertation he wrote on the sacred music of Nicolò Isouard, a Maltese composer born in the late eighteenth century. The dissertation involved producing a professional edition of Isouard's sacred music (something never done before), placing it in the setting of eighteenth-century Malta (still ruled at that time by the Knights of Malta) and evaluating it musically and theologically. John Griffiths, recently retired from a chair in music at the University of Melbourne, proved most generous and valuable as the co-director. I could never have taken on the task of directing Fra' Richard without constant help from this world-class musicologist.

Writing and publishing continue. In August, Connor Court put out the Australian edition of volume two of my memoirs, *On the Left Bank of the Tiber*. At two separate functions in Melbourne, Canon David Richardson (former director of the Anglican Centre in Rome) did the first launch and Tim Fischer (former Australian ambassador to the Holy See) did the second. Whatever you say about the usefulness or otherwise of book launches, they produce good parties with friends and relatives. Both volumes of the memoirs have now appeared in the UK, with Gracewing of Leominster.

One special blessing in 2013 was the chance of lunch with Grace de Mello, the sister of an outstanding Indian spiritual writer, Anthony de Mello, S.J., who died (of a heart attack) too young in 1987. A couple of years ago I worked with two American Jesuit friends, Dan Kendall and Jeff LaBelle in retrieving and publishing lectures by Tony on the *Spiritual Exercises* of St Ignatius Loyola. A former student of de Mello's ashram in Pune had kept copies of those lectures. The ravages of a tropical climate had given the thin, typed sheets the look of the Dead Sea Scrolls. Dan and Jeff succeeded in verifying the quotations and sources, despite challenges caused by Tony's normally quoting from memory.

All the blessings of the Christ Child.

7

Christmas 2014

"Lord God, as we rejoice in the birth of your Son, grant us the grace to affirm this great mystery with steadfast faith and to embrace it with an ever growing love.

We ask this in the name of Jesus, the Lord."

Prayer at Midnight Mass.

One happy milestone arrived in May when the University of Divinity (Melbourne) awarded Fra' Richard Divall a PhD for his thesis on the sacred music of an 18th century Maltese composer, Nicolò Isouard. After directing to completion over ninety doctoral dissertations at the Gregorian University (Rome), I did not intend to continue the role of *Doktorvater*. I am glad to have made three exceptions.[6] Richard, an outstanding conductor and editor of music, sacred and profane, has prepared a wonderful CD for the centenary of the Gallipoli campaign— or should we say tragedy?—in 2015. As the only professed Knight of

---

[6] The other two exceptions were Revd Simon Wayte, MGL (Missionaries of God's Love) and Daryl Barclay, a director of the choir at St Patrick's Cathedral, Melbourne. At the Australian National University in Canberra, Simon had already received a doctorate in astrophysics.

Malta in Australia, he constantly supports me as one of their three magistral chaplains in Melbourne. That involves frequently celebrating the Eucharist for the sick and elderly, along with leading the Knights and Dames of Malta on retreats, and celebrating the Eucharist with them and for them. When Richard drives me to age care centres, more often than not he fills his car with seventeenth- or eighteenth-century, Neapolitan music—the background to and nursery to the said Isouard.

One happy reunion came at an elaborate book launch in the Victorian State Library when Jay Winter presented the three volumes on World War I that he had edited for Cambridge University Press. I first met Jay in the sixties when we were both graduate students at Pembroke College, Cambridge. He has been a professor at Yale for years, and remains the epitome of a wise, gracious, and compassionate historian. He finds the homeless refugee to be *the* symbol of our times.

In early May I spoke at the Pumphouse, a pub in the inner-Melbourne suburb of Fitzroy, to a group of a hundred young people who meet for Theology at the Pub (to be distinguished from Spirituality in the Pub). They asked me to compare and contrast Pope John XXIII and Pope John Paul II, who had both just been canonized in Rome by Pope Francis on 27 April.

Lecturing trips have been limited to Victoria (specifically, the legendary gold-mining cities of Ballarat and Bendigo) and to various schools in the Lismore diocese (northern New South Wales). But in early July I did visit New Zealand and spoke to the priests, deacons, and seminarians in the Hamilton diocese. A centre, called Hobbiton, makes Tolkien's middle earth seem just around the corner. Through the filming of *The Lord of the Rings* and the arrival of tourists, the locals have enjoyed an unprecedented—there's that word again—additional prosperity.

For the year's most zestful human and spiritual experience, my vote has to go to three hundred members of the Calabrian community. In their centre just beyond the main Melbourne airport, I celebrated the Eucharist and led them in a procession (animated by a brass band) in honour of San Rocco. An unusual medieval saint, he cared for the sick up and down the Italian peninsula, caught the plague, but recovered. A large wound in his thigh reminds you of what he suffered.

Keep well and be blessed by the Christ Child and his Mother.

8

Christmas 2015

"God of splendor, at the birth of your incarnate Word, we are bathed in new radiance.

Grant that the light which shines in our hearts through faith may also show forth in our actions."

Prayer on Christmas day.

This year of grace, 2015, kept me for the most part in Australia. Before Easter I flew north to Singapore and lectured at a theological institute on Christ's resurrection. After Pentecost I went east to Wellington, New Zealand, and lectured on the Second Vatican Council to the clergy of the archdiocese. Otherwise, speaking engagements took me to Sydney, Brisbane, and other places in Eastern Australia: above all, three visits for meetings with educationalists and parents in the diocese of Lismore, Northern New South Wales. Ever since I returned to live in Melbourne in 2009, leaders in Catholic education in Lismore have invited me repeatedly to speak to them. To express my gratitude, I have dedicated to them *From Rome to Royal Park* (Connor Court/ Gracewing), volume three of my memoirs. It's number 65 of the books I have authored or co-authored since 1965.

The next book, *Revelation: Towards a Christian Theology of God's Self-revelation in Jesus Christ* (Oxford University Press; my twelfth with OUP), should be out before the end of 2016. By then, St Paul's (London) will have published a biblical work, *Letters to Nevie*, a book addressed to Genevieve ("Nevie") Peters, a grandniece of mine.

If I couldn't get to the USA and Europe, friends came from there to stay with me: most recently, Louis Caruana, SJ, the dean of philosophy at the Gregorian University (Rome). Louis included Melbourne in his lecture tour of Australia. A PhD from Cambridge, Louis is a philosopher of science and has insightful things to say about scientific method. During his visit to Oz, his chief base was the Australian National University (Canberra). Then Dan Kendall SJ, a long-standing friend from the University of San Francisco, came and stayed for ten days, enroute back to California from lecturing in Macau.

Landmarks punctuated the year: a 90th birthday celebration for my eldest sister Moira; the 80th birthday dinner for John Batt, a retired judge who has been a friend for sixty years (since we met as students of the classics, University of Melbourne). Both celebrations were held at the Melbourne Club.

The hospitality and empathy of family and friends provide more than enough support.

The present pope makes me think frequently of St Francis of Assisi, who created the first Christmas crib. He stamped on the world's imagination the place of Christ's birth—an outhouse for animals that is radiant with divine life.

9

Christmas 2016

"Today, O God of light, your loving-kindness dawns, your tender compassion shines upon us.

In our Savior, born of human flesh, you reveal your gracious gift of our birth to life eternal.

Fill us with wonder on this holy day. Let us treasure in our hearts what we have been told, so that our lives may proclaim your great and gentle mercy.

We ask this through Jesus Christ, your Word made flesh, who lives and rules with you in the unity of the Holy Spirit, in the splendor of eternal light, God for ever and ever."

Prayer on Christmas day.

This year's 400th anniversary of the death of William Shakespeare naturally brought celebrations and exhibitions around Melbourne. For me the most informative and enjoyable evening came with the power-point lecture (in English) by a visiting professor from the University of Padua, Alessandra Petrina, currently the president of the Italian Shakespeare Society. Sketching the difference between the University of Bologna (church-dominated) and the University of Padua (student-dominated), she teased out Shakespeare's great interest in Italy, in general, and his references to Padua, in particular. Her visit was sponsored by the Italian Assistance Association (CoAsIt, short for Comitato Assistenza Italiani) and the University of Melbourne.

Alessandra speaks perfect English but at the speed of a Ferrari. The lecture and dinner that followed proved tumultuous fun.

Alas, 2016 did not involve any visits for me to Italy or any elsewhere in Europe. In August, I did go as far as Auckland (New Zealand) and lectured to the clergy of that diocese on Pope Francis and his exhortation "the Joy of Love (*Amoris Laetitia).*" Since Auckland is closer than Perth (on the Western Australian coast), the trip to Auckland hardly felt like leaving Oz.

One bit of church news that proved very cheering concerned Blase Cupich, the Archbishop of Chicago being created a cardinal by Pope Francis. He studied with me at the Gregorian University (Rome). Later as rector of the Josephinum (Columbus, Ohio) he invited me to join Raymond Brown and Walter Kasper in speaking at a conference on Christian hope staged in that pontifical university. A few years ago Blase visited Melbourne on a lecturing tour of Australia, and we enjoyed a meal together at Newman College.

Sadly this year my dear friend, Richard Divall, has been increasingly invaded by cancer. A legendary conductor of Italian opera, he invited me in September 2015 to the opening night of "Mary Stuart." You will remember how at the end the lights go out and there is a terrible thud when Mary loses her head. This year Richard was to conduct another Donizetti opera, "Ann Boleyn," and I was looking forward to the horrible sound of a second such execution to round off the evening.

Occasional lectures filled up 2016; I also produced two books, *Revelation: Towards a Christian Interpretation of God's Self-revelation in Jesus Christ* (Oxford University Press) and *Letters to Nevie* (London, St Paul's) to encourage prayerful reading of the Scriptures. Around Easter 2017, Oxford University Press will publish my *Saint Augustine on the Resurrection of Christ*. What Augustine wrote and preached about the death of Jesus has attracted the attention of scholars. But, what he said on Christ's own resurrection precisely as such, there is very little, if any comment.

May the loving Jesus who lived, died, and rose to glory bless you always.

10

Christmas 2017

"Merciful God, grant that the Savior of the world, who was born this day to bring us new and divine existence, may bestow upon us the gift of life everlasting.

We ask this in the name of Jesus, the Lord."

Prayer for Christmas day.

On a visit years ago to Rome, Tennessee Williams spoke proudly of being descended from a brother of St Francis Xavier. While the saint died in the Far East, at least one of his siblings migrated to the Americas and became the ancestor of Williams.

"Life is saturated with death" was one of the memorable lines I recall from Williams, and it proved itself true in 2017. In January I preached at the funeral (in St Patrick's Cathedral and with a thousand people present) of Richard Divall and buried him in Melbourne General Cemetery. For twenty years the conductor of opera in Melbourne, Richard became a close friend after I returned to Melbourne in 2009 and began living at the Jesuit Theological College in Parkville only a few hundred metres from his home. In March I celebrated the funeral of my brother Jim, who for years had battled several forms of cancer. In October my sister Moira, the matriarch of our family, died suddenly and we buried her from the chapel of Newman College, where she had been married in 1946.

But the year was also full of life—not least the chance of christening Alexander and, a week later, Jonathan Charles, children of friends. For the first time in many years I attended a First Communion, that of two grandnieces (Susan and Naomi) at their school in Melbourne (called "Genazzano"). Eight tertians (Jesuits in their final year of formation), who came from China, India, Ireland, Japan, the Philippines, and Vietnam, arrived in January and departed in August. Much life also came through leading a spiritual retreat for a group of knights and dames of Malta (last March in Pymble, New South Wales) and a group of priests from the Armidale diocese (November in a motel near Coffs Harbour, also NSW). Right through the year, life came from keeping dementia at bay by writing: in April, Oxford University Press put out my *Saint Augustine on the Resurrection of Christ*; and then in October Liturgical Press published a book I wrote with John Wilkins, *Lost in Translation*. I have just finished dealing with an OUP copy-editor on a work to be released in July 2018, *Inspiration*.

Having written this about my experience of 2017, I am reminded of T. S. Eliot's question in "The Journey of the Magi": "Were we led all that way for Birth or Death?" Most years combine both, and 2017 did so in a particular way. There were three deaths (my brother Jim, my sister Moira, and Richard Divall), and four books were "born": *Inspiration* (OUP), *Tradition* (OUP), *A Christology of Religions* (Orbis Books), and *Moments of Grace* (Kevin Mayhew).

A blessed Christmas and grace-filled New Year to you and all your dear ones.

11

Christmas 2018

"God of wisdom and power, you established in the birth of your Son the source and fulfilment of all religion.

Number us among those who belong to Christ, for in him alone is salvation."

Prayer within the Octave of Christmas.

I am definitely at that time in life when every now and then you indulge big efforts to clean up correspondence and throw out all manner of old scraps. One recent binge unearthed a program for a degree ceremony at the University of Melbourne, 12 March 1958. Among the others receiving a degree (in fact, a MA in education) was Henry Leopold Speagle (what a splendid name!), who already had a MA in the faculty of arts. Long famous as a local specialist in matters liturgical, Henry celebrated his ninetieth birthday this year, and invited a group of friends to a suitable lunch of the "Ancient Anglicans" at the Melbourne Club.

That group meets at the Club every first Monday of the month. Their convenor is Alan Gregory, former Master of Ormond College

(University of Melbourne) and a very enthusiastic alumnus of Melbourne High School, the school where my Father happily did his final three years of secondary education. Ever since I returned to live in Melbourne in late 2009, the Ancient Anglicans have made me most welcome. Occasionally their archbishop, Philip Freier, who isn't that ancient, turns up. A couple of years back, I invited for lunch a visiting Catholic archbishop, George Stack (Cardiff, Wales). The AAs form a genial, relaxed, ecumenical forum.

The knights and dames of Malta continue to supply pastoral engagements: above all, a weekly Eucharist at a day-care centre for Italians and, every now and then, a more elaborate Eucharist (centred on Our Lady of Lourdes) in retirement homes and aged care centres around Melbourne. One of the knights or dames who joined me in those visits would assure the congregation: "If you are too old or sick to make a pilgrimage to Lourdes, we bring you right in your chapel Lourdes water and prayers that link you with the shrine."

Commitment to the cause of teaching the Latin and Greek languages and literature in Australian high schools and universities involves attending some lectures, including those delivered at formal lunches and dinners.

I am down to my last doctoral student, a candidate for the degree from the (ecumenical) University of Divinity, who is the choir director in the Melbourne cathedral, St Patrick's, and a very superior teacher of English literature at a leading high school. I feel myself to be an observer rather than a director of his dissertation (on Jean Pierre de Caussade's sacrament of the moment and a latter day "secular" counterpart in Virginia Woolf's *Mrs Dalloway*).

Last June, friends in the UK sponsored a weekend conference to commemorate the life and work of Michael Hayes, the beloved editor of *The Pastoral Review* who had died at Easter 2017. They flew me over to deliver the keynote lecture on Michael. Those few days in England let me catch up with relatives, friends at St Mary's University (to which Michael contributed so much), and a largish group who attended the summer reception of the London *Tablet* held in the courtyard of a church in Chelsea.

A blessed and very happy Advent, Christmas, and New Year.

12

Christmas 2019

"God of blessings, in the Holy Family you give us the model of a household drawn together in love.

Grant that we may follow their example and be welcomed with joy into your home in heaven."

Prayer for the feast of the Holy Family.

With tongue firmly in his cheek, the Irish genius James Joyce said of John Henry Newman: "nobody has ever written English prose that can be compared with that of a tiresome footling little Anglican parson who afterwards became a prince of the only true Church." It was a great joy to be alive for Newman's canonization on 13 October 2019. I hope and pray for a blazing exception to normal practice, and see Newman's writings prompt his entering a most select group of saints by being officially proclaimed the thirty-seventh Doctor of the Church.

My beloved sister Maev, the only other survivor of my parents' six children, was honored by Australian Catholic University with an honorary doctorate. I could not share that occasion on 12 April. But

I happily visited Canberra to celebrate her ninetieth birthday on 16 June, the famous Bloom's Day of Joyce's *Ulysses*.

As one of their chaplains, the Order of Malta keeps me pastorally engaged with visits to retirement homes around Melbourne and a respite centre for old Italians in Kew. At the end of November, along with Archbishop Jean Laffitte (their official prelate), several of the supreme council of the Order visited from Rome for an Asia Pacific Conference. Laffitte, when a student at the French Seminary, had been my student at the Gregorian University. After not seeing each other for 35 years, he hugged me and greeted me warmly as "professore."

As the sporting world knows, the annual Melbourne Cup is THE racing event in Australia. This year I attended the Mass—in fact concelebrated—for the racing fellowship in St Francis' Church, Melbourne's oldest, CBD church on 4 November, two days before the Cup (always held on the first Tuesday of November). Numerous owners, trainers, jockeys and other concerned folk attended the Mass. Some owners brought along the cups they had won in previous years; inside the sanctuary there was a special table for those trophies. The last time I attended the Cup Mass, Michelle Payne (see the film *Ride Like a Girl*) attended in her stylish jockey's outfit and was all set to win the Cup on an outsider (one hundred to one) two days later.

In early 2020 Oxford University Press will publish my *The Beauty of Jesus Christ*. Around the same time, Paulist Press (Mahwah, New Jersey) will release a book I have co-authored with Daniel Kendall: *Jesuits, Theology, and the American Catholic Church*.

Interest in my maternal grandfather is being promoted by the PM Glynn Institute of the Australian Catholic University. This year the institute published Anne Henderson's *Federation's Man of Letters* (Kapunda Press; Connor Court Publishing), which argued that Paddy Glynn's life, inspiration, intellectual heroes, and ideas remain powerfully relevant in debates that continue about Australia's identity and future. One of the founding fathers of Australian federation, until 1919 he remained in the national parliament and was a cabinet minister in several governments. In September, on the occasion of a visit to Australia, Archbishop Rowan Williams delivered in Sydney the annual PM Glynn lecture.

A blessed Christmas and every grace in the New Year.

13

Christmas 2020[7]

"Loving God, guardian of our homes, when you entrusted your Son to the care of Mary and Joseph, you did not spare them the pains that touch the life of every family.

Teach us to rely on your word, so that in our trials as in our joys we may be clothed in gentleness and patience and united in love.

Make us every thankful for the blessings you give us through Jesus Christ, your Word made flesh, who lives and rules with you in the unity of the Holy Spirit in the splendor of eternal light, God for ever and ever."

Prayer for the feast of the Holy Family.

Liebe Josef,

Congratulations on your 80th birthday, and many thanks for all the news—about Hanna spending a year in the US, Marie's Masters,

---

[7] The Christmas letter of 2020 survived in what I wrote to two long-standing German friends, Josef and Ingrid Nolte (who lived in the university town of Tübingen, south of Stuttgart). Hanna and Marie are their grand-children.

and the rest. All the best, Josef, as you write your memoirs. Yes, our early years are decisive and, in many ways, the most interesting part of our story.

Last Wednesday I was discharged from hospital, after 35 days of battling a thyroid gland run amok and affecting my heart. Now I face the grind of daily exercises—rehabilitation as they call it.

A couple of months ago, Paulist Press (Mahwah, New Jersey) published a work I co-authored, *Jesuits, Theology and the American Catholic Church*. Some time in 2021, Paulist Press will put out my *Illuminating the New Testament*—my last book, I expect. [It wasn't.]

My warm thanks to you and Ingrid for being such wonderful friends. In many ways you have enriched my life, and I am most grateful.

Here in Melbourne we still live very prudently. I can hardly imagine what post-vaccine existence will be like.

Peace, love and good cheer to you and all your dear ones for Christmas and the New Year, and good Lord's blessing be upon you abundantly,

14

Christmas 2021

"As your sons and daughters, O loving God, we come before you in thanksgiving, called and united by your eternal Word.

Teach us to ponder the mystery of Nazareth, so that we may always find in you the source of our strength and the unity of our families."

Prayer for the feast of the Holy Family.

I hope and pray that all is going at least tolerably well for you. Here on Royal Parade, I ply myself with sayings from Pope Francis (e.g. "faith is not a light which scatters all our darkness but a lamp which guides our steps") and the motto of Xavier Jesuit School Cambodia ("Dare to dream of a brighter future"). I find that motto courageous and moving, especially after hearing from Jesuit friends who work in South-East Asia. They persistently picture Cambodia as the most difficult and dangerous mission in that part of the world.

During the mini-break that came just before the extreme

lockdown, a young couple were married in our chapel here at the Jesuit Theological College. They turned up the other day with their lasting thanks in the form of a largish bush. With the help of Ai, one of our Vietnamese priests, I planted it in the front garden, right outside 159 Royal Parade and facing the steady flow of students (of Melbourne University) and nurses (from the Royal Melbourne Hospital) who continue to make their masked way up and down Royal Parade.

I continue to miss my dear Californian friend, Dan Kendall. After his passing the department of theology and religious studies at the University of San Francisco held a memorial service for Dan. He had been on the faculty there since 1979. Marion [Peters] stood in for me, and read what I wanted to say about Dan, my first doctoral student in Rome and one with whom I did a lot of publishing over the years. Marion and her husband Rick were good friends of Dan, and sometimes visited the USF Jesuit residence for brunch on Sundays.[8]

Recently I tried out the TV series "Grantchester"—an act of pure nostalgia since, while the young vicar is stationed a few miles out of Cambridge, most of the action takes place at the University and, specifically, at Newnham College (with, in this case, both the victim and the killer being students there). Among the alumnae of Newnham, Emma Thomson, Germaine Greer and my cousin Jane Ellison would all have been tempted to extreme language if

---

8   A world-standing hepatologist, Marion is my eldest niece, the daughter of my deceased sister Moira.

they happened to have seen this instalment. It's not that several students from St John's College came out better. But there was no need to rubbish Newnham in that way.

May Jesus, Mary and Joseph bless you in every way at Christmas and into the New Year.

15

Christmas 2022

"Bind our families together and deepen our faith, so that, like the Holy Family of Nazareth, we may grow in wisdom, obedient to your word."

Prayer for the feast of the Holy Family.

Dear relatives and friends, the easing-out-of-the Covid year provided us Melbournians with a cold and damp winter. Here at the Jesuit Theological College in Parkville, a Tawny Frogmouth couple (cousins to owls) did us proud by nesting in a large oak that fills one side of our back garden. After teaching their chick to perch motionless on a branch, they all decamped, instead of becoming our most welcome permanent residents. A magpie couple partly made up our loss by producing two offspring, which squawk ceaselessly to reveal an insatiable hunger. The parents generously feed them with the worms that welcomed the wet weather—only to die at the end of a beak. Mum and dad magpie never show the slightest sign of irritation at the impatience of their two youngsters.

The October rains left a nearby football field under water, and was quickly visited by a large flock of ibises. They waded around gorging themselves for a couple of days.

It's a certainty that if we met, or when we meet face to face, you would/will ask me about writing plans for 2023. Carl Gustav Jung, the Swiss psychologist who celebrated everywhere the number four, would be delighted that the immediate plans are fourfold:

** Check the proofs and indices of *The Spiritual Exercises of St Ignatius of Loyola* (to be published by Paulist Press (Mahwah, NJ) in early 2023);

** See through the press with Connor Court Publishing (Brisbane) *Letters to Maev* (letters I wrote to my beloved sister Maev between 1978 and 2017).

** Find a publisher for the book I am preparing with a young poet, Manfred Cain, commentaries on the Gospel poems published in Peter Steele's *Raining Angels.*

** To prepare with two French-speaking Jesuits, Marc and Jean-Marc, a book on revelation according to Christianity, Judaism, and Islam. Jean-Marc won't be able to complete his contribution before next June. This book could at the earliest see the light of day in 2024.

Every blessing to you and all your dear ones for Christmas and the New Year, Gerald.

16

Christmas 2023

"As your sons and daughters, O loving God, we come before you in thanksgiving, called and united by your eternal Word.

Teach us to ponder the mystery of Nazareth, so that we may always find in you the source of our strength and the unity of our families."

Prayer for the feast of the Holy Family.

My affectionate Christmas greetings to all your dear family. Recently I felt a tad flattered to discover that I had inspired a poem by Peter Steele, SJ, which appeared in his 2008 collection, *White Knight with Beebox*. Peter never pretended to be another Gerard Manley Hopkins, but he has been the top poet so far produced by the Australian Jesuits. He also wrote on Jonathan Swift, and lectured at Oxford on autobiography. One day back in the 1980s or even in the 1970s, Peter mentioned over lunch a phrase that I had used in some publication ("beyond question" as a synonym for "unquestionably"). The phrase impressed him, but he cautioned me against using it too often. Now I have found that the phrase turned up as a title and subject for a poem in the 2008 collection. Peter expounded ironically the "blessings" brought to a society that decided to abolish the use of questions and existed "beyond question". Now some items I may have already shared with you.

Reading or re-reading the works of Peter has been "thrust upon me" by discovering in two Melbourne archives a wonderful correspondence between him and the Nobel laureate Seamus Heaney: 33 letters from SH and 23 from Peter. Unfortunately, lodging on this trove came too late for me to pass them on to Christopher Reid who in October 2023 published with Faber & Faber an over 800-page book of selected letters by SH. But a day for the Heaney/Steele correspondence will come, when the Heaney family flashes the green light of publication.

If Reid's volume has not a word to or about Peter Steele, some Australians creep in: Les Murray (the bard from the bush, pp. 202-03), Chris Wallace-Crabbe, a colleague of Steele (and fellow poet) in the English department of the University of Melbourne (pp. 365-66), and Clive James (whose poetry grew richer the longer he lived, p. 247). There is a witty letter from SH to a former missionary priest who came from Melbourne, Joe Broderick, son of a famous trainer, Wally, whose horses won the Melbourne Cup, 'the race that stops the nation', ten or twelve times. Joe was one of the translators into Spanish of SH's poetry. He lived for some years in Colombia and wrote on Samuel Beckett (pp. 788-89).

Among other things, SH's letter to Joe discussed some modern films and the acting of Daniel Day-Lewis.

Minor celebrations here in Melbourne for the centenary of W. B. Yeats's receiving the Nobel prize in 1923 finally explained for me how and why the Irish poet (from grandfather Glynn's home town of Gort) brought Mother and Father together. That same year of 1923 lots of folk of Irish extraction, like my parents, were frequently talking to each other about Yeats at the University and elsewhere in Melbourne. When he became engaged, my father acknowledged his debt in a simple ditty ("O Yeats, if you but knew…"). The Irish poet proved the first in the triad of Irish winners: Yeats, Beckett, and Heaney. Or should we add George Bernard Shaw, who grew up in Ireland, moved to live in England, and received a Nobel prize in 1925?

Much love and grace for Christmas and the New Year to you and all your dear ones, and long live what for me, in the face of the international horrors, has been a sumptuous poetry year.

Epilogue:

Cicero and the Wider Context

My fifteen Christmas letters fit within the context of Pauline patronage. We should not forget their wider, secular context. The humanities, along with Christian faith, bookend any recourse to the literary form of letters.

The correspondence (68–44 BC) between the Roman orator, philosopher, and politician Marcus Tullius Cicero and his friend Titus Pomponius Atticus provides a rich, even unique source of information about the period when the Roman Republic fell, the Empire emerged, and Christianity was born. Cicero revealed himself and his views of contemporary events and political figures in a remarkably frank way which meant that the collection of more than 900 letters was not published until years after his death. I am no Cicero, and not in danger if I publish letters during my lifetime. But sometimes I wonder whether my commitment to writing and collecting letters has been, at least in part, unconsciously prompted by unease over a period of world history when democracies are falling apart and oligarchies or worse are emerging.

Grandfather's Letters

I started gathering and publishing letters years ago. It was not enough to write a life of my maternal grandfather, Patrick McMahon Glynn (1855–1931) and put out his biography in 1965 with Melbourne University Press and Cambridge University Press. Within a decade, letters followed. Polding Press published *Patrick McMahon Glynn: Letters to his Family (1874–1927)* in 1974. His first letter describes his pilgrimage as a nineteen-year-old to the shrine of the Virgin Mary at Lourdes in southern France. On Sunday 23 August 1934, he wrote to his mother from the Hotel due Prince Albert, Paris:

"I returned yesterday night from Lourdes, and was too tired to write to you as I was thirty hours in the train. The pilgrimage was very large, there being upward of 1500 pilgrims from Paris, besides 2000 from Nimes whom we met at Lourdes. Lourdes is very prettily situated among a range of hills which run from the Pyrenees, and nearly entirely consists of religious bookshops, lodging houses, and hotels. I found it very hard to get a bed, but at last managed to get half another fellow's. I drank the water, and took a bath, and feel somewhat better, but as there were only eight persons cured out of the whole 3,500, I could not expect to be one of the number, as they were models of piety and holiness. I bleed a great deal from the nose now and then but not much in the last few days; I think it has done my head good. Everything is astir here in Paris—same as every other day, theatres, shops etc. all open.

I have some photographs of Lourdes which will give you an idea of what it is. I gave ten shillings to the Curé of Lourdes to say one Mass for Papa and another for myself. You will be surprised to hear [that] none of the priests or people at Lourdes speak English, and even can't hear a foreigner's confession without special permission, but I managed to get confession. I hope you are all well, and with fond love your affectionate son, Patrick Glynn."[9]

Mostly grandfather's letters came from the years after he sailed to Australia in 1880. Settling in South Australia, he began practicing as a lawyer and entered state politics. He took part as an elected delegate in drafting the Australian federal constitution, and was elected to the national House of Representatives in 1901. After serving as a minister in three Commonwealth governments, he was defeated in the 1919 elections, being the last of the "founding fathers" to sit in the Commonwealth Parliament.

My family was delighted that Brenda Niall and her co-editor of the 1998 *Oxford Book of Australian Letters* included the letter Paddy Glynn wrote proposing marriage during the Federal Convention that produced the Australian constitution, He enlivened proceedings at the (1987) Second Session by suddenly risking "the inevitable question" with Abigail Dynon of Melbourne, rushing down from Sydney to marry her (with a legendary fellow politician King O'Malley being the principal witness), and then returning at once with his bride to the

---

[9] *Patrick McMahon Glynn: Letters to His Family (1874–1927)*, ed. Gerald Glynn O'Collins, SJ, (Melbourne: Polding Press, 1974), 2–3. The Australian National Library (Canberra) holds the original copies of all these letters.

proceedings of the Convention.[10] On 13 September 1897 he wrote to his mother announcing the news:

"My dear Mother, We are again in the thick of the Federal Convention work, the Second or Sydney sitting being now on. It is to consider the amendments suggested by the various Australian parliaments to the bill drafted by the First, the Adelaide Convention. I accomplished rather a record last week. On Tuesday, during the sitting, I wrote a proposal of marriage to a girl whom I had only spoken to once, had a telegram accepting on Wednesday, made what the audience considered a great speech on Thursday at 5.30 p.m., took the 7.15 Express to Melbourne same night, got married on Saturday & returned same day, arriving here on Sunday.

You will think I am mad. Perhaps a little, but it may have saved me from a reckless step. She is at all events what will please you, a Catholic, a good one, with enough religion for the two of us. She has been around Europe several times, & spoke French to the Pope for half an hour. I believe she is well off, but I'm hanged if I know and didn't care. I hope I won't pull her down from Heaven. But the bell rings the House together again, so I must, with love, say good bye, your affectionate Son, P. McM. Glynn."[11]

The letter of proposal of 7 September 1897 had run as follows:

---

[10] An American-born, Australian politician, King O'Malley (1858–1953) was a member of the Labor Party and would become twice Minister for Home Affairs in the federal government. He was not, however, a member of the federal convention that prepared the Australian convention.
[11] Ibid., 171.

"Dear Miss Dynon, I suppose it would do poor justice to the reputation my country-men bear for courage—though in this case it may be called audacity—if I did not risk, as so many others in other cases have, with better or worse fortune done, the inevitable question. The world is made up of incompatibles, or rather contradictions. Without the union of opposites there would be no possibility of the average that makes for progress. I am, in most of the qualities that build a character, at one pole, you at the other, but your sex is born to redeem, and Goodness Knows there is a big field for redemption in my case. Well, you can well think that I am, for once at all events in my life, in a bit of a muddle. I have written pamphlets, leading articles, essays etc., by the mile, but never before put in writing the impertinence of a proposal of marriage. And this has to be done, at the table of the Legislative Assembly of New South Wales, with the Federal Convention sitting, and Mr Lyne, within a yard of me, pouring on the too-thinly-protected top of my head, a Niagara of figures.[12] However, I must attempt it.

Well, Dear Miss Dynon, to be candid, which indeed is my dearest desire, I heard of you six or seven years ago, and from what a lady said who knew you well said of you then, I know, if on meeting you I did not feel it instinctively, that you are deserving of the reputation you bear as I am under the estimate many, or rather some of my generous friends, in Kindness form of me. I say this because it will tell you at once, that I cannot possibly understand you. You unfortunately—or rather, perhaps, fortunately for myself—know

---

[12] Sir William Lyne (1844–1913), a premier of New South Wales and, after federation, a federal cabinet minister.

little of me; that is, outside my reputation as a public man. But as far as I can say it, I feel that I am Bohemian in temperament, fond of the softer—I don't like to say poetic—side of life; liable, like many of my romantic countrymen, to extremes of spirit, by no means correct as the world goes, but at all events capable of discerning, if not following, the Right. The girl that takes me will deserve an indulgence—a dispensation from purgatory, so that I may have at least a negative recommendation.

But I find, with my usual want of pluck in matters outside my line, I am becoming all preface. The Sum of it all is this, if you consent to marry me, Miss Dynon, you will, for the sacrifice, deserve Heaven, and probably save me from somewhere else. May I ask you to do so. I am by no means well off—but why should I say that to you?—but I can and do work, and though, if I may use the term for its expressiveness, devil-may-care in most matters, will try under the great responsibility, to become financially orthodox. I don't care the proverbial rap for the Ceremonial side of life.

If you consent to become my wife—a great word—why should we not be married at once? It will have the advantage for me that the matter will be inevitably settled before you know too much of me. It is a great occasion here. I have plenty of friends here now, and, though a bit of a reprobate in Religion, an aunt, Superioress of the Sisters of St Joseph, who would back me up if necessary.[13] And she reminds me of one, who gives a relative merit to her son. I have a Mother that, apart from prejudice, I can from the bottom of my heart say, is, as my aunt said on Sunday, a saint, if ever a woman, who is no narrow puritan, can be one. I never yet met a man or woman that did not respect her disposition; an able, self-sacrificing, as well as human and feminine woman.

If you have me, I can honestly promise you to give you no divided heart, and to live no double life. You will know me, for good or bad, as I am.

Well, if you will bless me, I will with your consent, go for you on Friday, marry on Saturday, and return same day. If you will come—anyhow I wish you would—over at once, so much the better. We can be married on the arrival of the train. My friend Mr O'Malley will give me away; I hope he has not done so already. This is lot to ask, but the occasion is my great excuse. I am not my own master now—we are servants of the Nation and its destinies. Besides as I said, I know you thoroughly—and after we can call one another wife and husband, well what does the unorthodox way of settling the bond matter?

---

[13] Grace Walsh (known in her religious institute as Mother Bernard) (1837–98) was a sister of Paddy Glynn's mother. For some years she lived in Sydney and led the Sisters of St Joseph, replacing for 1885–98 the now canonized foundress, Mother Mary MacKillop (1842–1909). Having joined Mother Mary's community in 1868, Grace was one of her first companions. For the final decade of her life (1899–1909), Mother Mary returned as superior general of her religious institute.

In Hopes of a reply that will enable me to really begin to live, I am, Dear Miss Dynon, your admirer and friend under any circumstances, P. McM. Glynn.

The Letters of Others

Publishing letters has continued to our day. Let me name a few examples.

In 2015, *The War Letters of Sir John Monash* appeared. My father had served with him on the French front during the First World War. The particular success of this collection of letters encouraged me to be even more interested in letters both as a form of literature and a source for historical writing.

Letters to Camondo by Edmund de Waal, the bestselling author of *The Hare with Amber Eyes*, came out in 2021 and has increased my admiration of letters as an art form. Finally, 2022 witnessed the publication of the correspondence between the American writer and political activist Robert Ellsberg and the English hermit and art critic Sister Wendy Beckett. Both of these recent publications deserve their success and have confirmed my passion for publishing letters.

In 2016, St Paul's Publishing (London) put out my *Letters to Nevie*. This grandniece, Genevieve ("Nevie") Peters, whom I christened back in 2000, has acted as my muse in letter writing. She was the recipient of one letter in *Letters from Rome and Beyond* (Connor Court Publishing, 2021). *Letters from the Pandemic* (Connor Court

Publishing, 2022) contained other letters to her and ten letters by her.

An American poet, Randall Jarrell (1914–1965), said: "Writing poetry well is only occasionally difficult; usually it's impossible." Could what Randall Jarrell said of poetry be applied to writing letters? Writing letters well is only occasionally difficult; usually it's impossible.

A friend of mine used to talk often of situations being "fraught"— fraught with risk, danger, or at least the possibility of undesirable outcomes. Fraught situations are those that, even (or especially) unintentionally, can cause anxiety and distress. Choosing and editing letters for publication create such risks. (See the remarks below that come from Stephanie MacGillivray.)

Those who read my latest three volumes of letters (all with Connor Court Publishing) could well ask: Where are the letters *from* his sister Maev? She was a great friend and companion in my life. She did send me many astonishing letters during her years in New York and later in Port Moresby. Why did I fail to keep those letters? I have no ready explanation.

The failure looks even worse when I recall the example of our beloved elder sister Moira (Peters). She kept *everything*, even the boarding passes for international flights she took over the years with her dear husband, Jim Peters.

Yes, writing letters well is only occasionally difficult; usually it's impossible. But it's always worth trying to write letters well.

Whatever else you achieve, you show that you respect, and even love, the person you are writing to. In any case, you will be doing your best to keep up the public standard of the English language.

Christmas letters enjoy, however, an exemption from the rules for writing "proper" letters—the right to include one sentimental story. In the course of Christian history, the accounts of the nativity from Matthew and Luke have proved themselves eminently sentimental. And let's not forget or disparage that frequent way of communicating to us God's loving friendship. To show what I have in mind, let me insert one such story:

One winter's day, a small boy was standing on a grate next to a bakery trying to keep his shoeless feet warm. A woman passing by saw the frosty-toed child and her heart went out to him. He wore only a light-weight jacket and no shoes; and the air was chilly, the wind sharp. "Where are your shoes, young man," she asked. The boy reluctantly admitted he didn't have any. "Why don't you come with me and we'll see what we can do about that," the woman said. Taking his hand, she led him to a nearby department store, and bought him a new pair of shoes and a warm jacket.

When they came out onto the street, the little boy was so excited that he immediately began to run off and show his family the gifts. Suddenly he stopped, turned around and ran back to the woman. He thanked her and then hesitated: "Ma'am, could I ask you a question? Ma'am, are you God's wife?" The woman smiled and said: "Oh, no, I'm not God's wife, just one of God's children." The small boy grinned and nodded enthusiastically: "I knew it! I just knew you were related!" [Anonymous]

Appendix:

A Review of *Letters to Maev* by Stephanie Macgillivray[14]

"There will always be debate about whether the publication of one's own letters is an act of generosity or arrogance. There are difficult choices involved: does one publish the correspondence received in return? Does one edit? Does one explain? Or, as with any publication, does one just accept that you will never satisfy all readers, and hope that at least some might appreciate your words?

Letters to Maev contains the letters from the period 1978-2017 of Gerald O'Collins, an Australian Jesuit priest based for many years at the Gregorian University in Rome, written to his sister Maev, an educator and social worker who spent many years working with communities in Papua New Guinea.

This book is many things: a commentary on social and political change, an endearing lens into a loving, long-distance sibling relationship, and a window into the intriguing world of the Catholic Church and life in the city of Rome.

[14] S. MacGillivray, review of G. O'Collins, *Letters to Maev: a theologian and his sister* (Brisbane, Australia: Connor Court Publishing, 2023)

It is an unfortunate (and sadly, often true) stereotype that priests often cut a lonely figure; but Gerald O'Collins safely contradicts this image. His colourful Roman life spans from evenings in the Doria Pamphilj Palace with the Prince and Princess ("Frank and Orietta"), to being driven back to the Gregorian University one afternoon in a diplomatic car after "lunch with the Lawlers" – Sir Peter Lawler being the Australian Ambassador to the Holy See at the time.

When not enjoying esteemed company in the Eternal City, O'Collins spent much time travelling the globe on academic pursuits, as well as always finding time to catch up with his impressive collection of family, friends and acquaintances, seemingly strategically situated in each of the places he visits.

However, it's not all glamour. One letter which stands out is written during Gerald's visit to Colombia, in which he recounts his visit with true feeling for the people he meets and their struggles. One can't help but feel that it is Maev's influence on Gerald which gives his writing such sensitivity and compassion.

We don't see Maev's responses. At first I wanted to know how she reacted to her brother's slightly surreal life, but in fact the book is better without them. It pays homage to Maev through Gerald's words, and that's enough.

Gerald's letters to Maev are incredibly funny, interesting and poignant. For anyone with even the smallest interest in workings of the Catholic Church in its "headquarters", this book is essential reading. O'Collins' sense of humour is dry, but never flippant. His deep faith and conviction (especially and interestingly about the resurrection) give him the authority to make observational quips about the quirky nature of life in this institution. For those of us who work in this environment, Gerald's tales are very relatable, insightful and entertaining beyond measure.

Reading this book shows us that with a little care and a lot of love, the strength of a human bond can withstand any distance; that when a discerning thinker publishes their own correspondence, it really can be a gift; and that we must never let the art form of letter-writing die out.

Most of all, it makes you want to write a letter."

Index of Names